TEAM SPIRIT ®

SMART BOOKS FOR YOUNG FANS

30 ▸    20 ▸    10 ▸

# THE TENNESSEE TITANS

## BY
## MARK STEWART

New Hanover County Public Library
201 Chestnut Street
Wilmington, North Carolina 28401

NORWOOD HOUSE 🏠 PRESS

CHICAGO, ILLINOIS

Norwood House Press
P.O. Box 316598
Chicago, Illinois 60631

For information regarding Norwood House Press, please visit our website at:
www.norwoodhousepress.com or call 866-565-2900.

All photos courtesy of Getty Images except the following:
Icon SMI (4), Topps, Inc. (6, 16, 17, 20, 34 both, 37, 38, 42 both),
Black Book Partners (10, 11, 14, 21, 23, 26, 27, 28, 35 all, 36, 41, 43 both),
Houston Oilers (15, 33, 45), Palisades Publications (40), Matt Richman (48).
Cover Photo: Tom DiPace

The memorabilia and artifacts pictured in this book are presented for educational and informational purposes,
and come from the collection of the author.

Editor: Mike Kennedy
Designer: Ron Jaffe
Project Management: Black Book Partners, LLC.
Special thanks to Topps, Inc.

Library of Congress Cataloging-in-Publication Data

Stewart, Mark, 1960-
  The Tennessee Titans / by Mark Stewart. -- Rev. ed.
    p. cm. -- (Team spirit)
  Includes bibliographical references and index.
  Summary: "A revised Team Spirit Football edition featuring the Tennessee
Titans that chronicles the history and accomplishments of the team. Includes
access to the Team Spirit website which provides additional information and
photos"--Provided by publisher.
  ISBN 978-1-59953-542-5 (library edition : alk. paper) -- ISBN
978-1-60357-484-6 (ebook)
  1.  Tennessee Titans (Football team)--History--Juvenile literature.  I.
Title.
  GV956.T45S74 2012
  796.332'640976855--dc23
                                        2012016235

Manufactured in the United States of America in North Mankato, Minnesota.
205N—082012

**COVER PHOTO**: The Titans get ready to make a defensive stand.

# Table of Contents

**ABOUT OUR GLOSSARY**

In this book, there may be several words that you are reading for the first time. Some are sports words, some are new vocabulary words, and some are familiar words that are used in an unusual way. All of these words are defined on page 46. Throughout the book, sports words appear in **bold type**. Regular vocabulary words appear in ***bold italic type***.

# Meet the Titans

A game is never over until the final play. The Tennessee Titans and their fans know this better than anyone. Some of their most thrilling victories have come when the last few seconds were ticking away. That is why no team plays harder from the opening kickoff until the game is over.

The Titans are known for their strong and speedy players. Tennessee fans cheer just as loud for a crushing block or a teeth-rattling tackle as they do for a long run or diving catch. After a game with the Titans, opponents are guaranteed to have a few more bumps and bruises than usual.

This book tells the story of the Titans. They have been playing spirited football for more than 50 years. The team has always been built around a group of stars with major skills and big personalities. The Titans then surround them with hardworking players who do their jobs well. That formula has been Tennessee's recipe for success.

The Titans congratulate Jason Jones after a good defensive play. Tennessee loves players with great skills and big personalities.

# Glory Days

**BILLY CANNON**
HOUSTON OILERS    HALFBACK

**W**hen a *professional* football team picks a name, it usually sticks with it forever. In fact, of all the teams that were playing in 1960, only three have changed their names, including the Tennessee Titans. From 1960 to 1998, they were called the Oilers. From 1960 to 1996, they played in Houston, Texas. The Oilers were original members of the **American Football League (AFL)**. Team owner Bud Adams helped the new league get its start.

Adams knew that the AFL had to grab headlines in order to attract fans. Most people loved the **National Football League (NFL)**. The AFL needed to make a splash. Adams did his part when he signed Billy Cannon, the nation's greatest college football star. Cannon chose the Oilers because Adams offered him twice as much money as any NFL team was willing to pay.

Adams made another good move by signing George Blanda to be the team's quarterback and kicker. He had been a member of the Chicago Bears in the NFL for many years. Blanda became a star in Houston and led the Oilers to the **AFL Championship Game** three times. They won in 1960 and 1961, and lost a thrilling double-**overtime** battle in 1962. They reached the AFL Championship Game again in 1967.

The Oilers were an exciting club in their early years. In 1961,

they scored 513 points to set a pro football record. Houston often beat opponents with its great passing game. Blanda's favorite receivers were Bill Groman, Charlie Hennigan, and Charlie Tolar. Houston's defense could also win games. Tony Banfield, Freddy Glick, Don Floyd, and Ed Husmann were among the top players in the early days of the AFL.

**LEFT**: Billy Cannon was the first college star to join the AFL.
**ABOVE**: George Blanda drops back to pass.

The Oilers had some good teams in the 1970s and 1980s. By then, the AFL and NFL had **merged**, and Houston became part of the NFL's **American Football Conference (AFC)**. The team's offensive stars included quarterbacks Dan Pastorini and Warren Moon, receivers Ernest Givins, Haywood Jeffires, and Drew Hill, and kicker Toni Fritsch. Elvin Bethea, Ken Houston, Curley Culp, and Robert Brazile led the defense.

Houston's best player was Earl Campbell. He was a powerful runner who battered opponents with his bruising style. Campbell topped the NFL in rushing each season from 1978 to 1980.

In the early 1990s, Houston fans believed their club could reach the **Super Bowl**, but disaster always seemed to strike in the **playoffs**. In 1997, Adams decided it was time to rebuild and moved the Oilers to Tennessee. Two years later, they opened a new stadium in Nashville and became the Titans.

**LEFT**: Earl Campbell outruns the Kansas City defense.
**ABOVE**: Warren Moon and Haywood Jeffires

Tennessee relied on three rugged offensive stars quarterback Steve McNair, running back Eddie George, and tight end Frank Wycheck. The defense was even tougher. It starred Jevon Kearse, Samari Rolle, and Blaine Bishop. In 1999, behind great seasons from McNair and George, Tennessee reached the Super Bowl for the first time.

Age and injuries caught up with the Titans in the years that followed. By the end of 2005, seven **Pro Bowl** players who had been on the 1999 team were no longer on the roster. Coach Jeff Fisher didn't panic. He was able to work wonders with a lineup full of *veterans* and young stars. Travis Henry, Alge Crumpler, and Kerry Collins joined the club. All had been cast off by other teams. Meanwhile, Bo Scaife, Vince Young, Albert Haynesworth, Cortland Finnegan, and Keith Bulluck were given a chance to shine.

In 2008, a **rookie** named Chris Johnson joined the Titans. He gave them the exciting "big play" running back they needed to win the close games. In Johnson's first season, he and LenDale White combined for more than 2,000 yards. The Titans finished the season with the best record in the NFL!

The Titans know that they cannot rest on their past success. They now play in the **AFC South**—the same **division** as the Indianapolis Colts, Houston Texans, and Jacksonville Jaguars. These teams play one another twice each season. One bad bounce or one mental error can mean the difference between winning and losing.

**LEFT**: Steve McNair
**ABOVE**: Chris Johnson

# Home Turf

**W**hen the team started as the Oilers, it played in several stadiums. None of them could compare to Houston's famous Astrodome. The Oilers were the first pro football team to call a domed stadium its home. They played in the Astrodome for 30 years starting in 1968.

After the team moved to Tennessee in 1997, it spent two seasons in college stadiums until construction on a new home in Nashville was finished. The stadium opened in 1999. It is located on the Cumberland River. It has had a couple of different names over the years, but most fans call it the Coliseum. The Titans have sold out every game since they moved there.

## BY THE NUMBERS

- The Titans' stadium has 69,143 seats.
- The stadium cost $290 million to build.
- In May of 2010, flooding in Nashville dumped six feet of water on the field.

Fans watch the Titans play on a sunny fall Sunday in Nashville.

# Dressed for Success

**O**il is big business in Houston. When the team played there, its helmet featured a picture of an oil derrick—a piece of equipment used for drilling. The team also used a *logo* with a picture of an oiler, or oil worker. The Oilers became the Titans after moving to Tennessee. A titan is even larger than a giant. That name had been used in the early 1960s by the New York team that is now called the Jets.

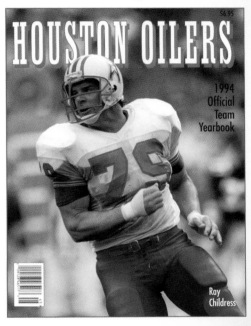

While the Titans changed their name, they stayed true to other team *traditions* that started in Houston. Tennessee's main color—light blue—has been the same since 1960. The Oilers also used red and white. Tennessee features those colors, too, along with dark blue. The team has worn three different helmet colors over the years—blue, silver, and white.

**LEFT**: Rob Bironas gets ready to kick off in Tennessee's home uniform.
**RIGHT**: Ray Childress models the old Oilers uniform on the cover of the 1994 yearbook.

# We Won!

The Oilers were one of the top teams in the AFL. They were champions of the league's **Eastern Division** four times from 1960 to 1967. The Oilers took the AFL championship twice, in 1960 and 1961.

In the 1960 AFL Championship Game, Houston hosted the Los Angeles Chargers. On this day, George Blanda did it all for the

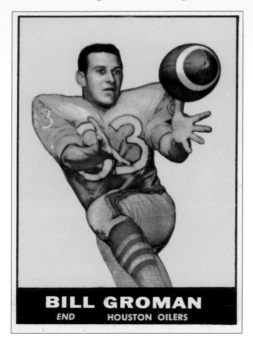

**BILL GROMAN**
END    HOUSTON OILERS

Oilers. After the Chargers went ahead 6–0, Blanda threw a touchdown pass and then kicked a **field goal** to give the Oilers a 10–9 lead at halftime. He struck again in the third quarter with a scoring toss to Bill Groman. Los Angeles responded with a touchdown of its own.

Early in the fourth quarter, Blanda and the Oilers started a drive near their own goal line. He threw a short pass to Billy Cannon, who broke a tackle and outran

**LEFT**: Bill Groman caught a scoring pass for Houston in the first AFL title game.
**RIGHT**: George Blanda led the Oilers to two AFL crowns.

HOUSTON

GEORGE BLANDA quarterback

the rest of the defense for an 88-yard touchdown. The Chargers mounted two drives into Houston territory, but the Oilers stopped them on fourth down twice—the last time with less than a minute to play. The Oilers celebrated their first AFL championship with a 24–16 victory.

One year later, the same teams met again. The first game had been played in Houston. This time, the Oilers traveled to San Diego. The Chargers had moved there before the season began. San Diego fans watched a wild contest that included seven **fumbles** and 10 **interceptions**.

The Oilers held a slim 3–0 lead in the third quarter. With the ball in San Diego territory, Blanda was forced to scramble. When he looked downfield, he saw Cannon break open. Blanda lofted a high pass that Cannon somehow managed to snag. He then dodged

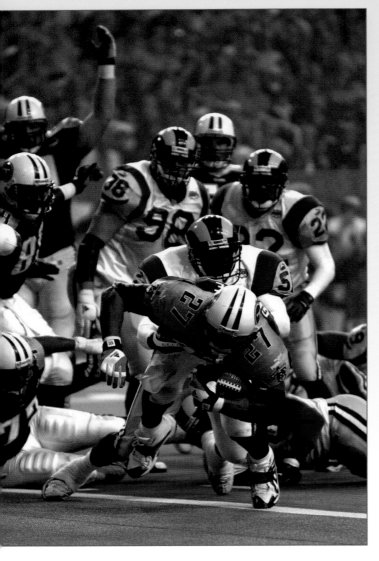

a tackler and sprinted into the end zone for a spectacular 35-yard touchdown.

The Chargers cut the lead to 10–3 in the fourth quarter. With two minutes left, San Diego marched down the field, hoping to tie the game. Julian Spence stopped the drive with an interception. Once again, the Oilers held on for the AFL championship.

Houston played in another thrilling championship game in 1962. This time, they faced the Dallas Texans. Blanda led a furious fourth-quarter comeback to tie the score 17–17. Unfortunately, the Texans kicked a field goal to win in double-overtime.

Nearly four *decades* later, the Titans were part of another spectacular championship game. In 1999, with Steve McNair and Eddie George leading the way, Tennessee made the playoffs and won the AFC championship. The Titans met the St. Louis Rams in Super Bowl XXXIV. Few people gave Tennessee a chance to win.

It looked like they were right after the Rams grabbed a 16–0 lead. The Titans refused to quit and battled back on a pair of touchdown runs by George. He finished as the game's top rusher with 92 yards. With three minutes left, Tennessee tied the score. The Rams responded with a long touchdown to regain the lead.

McNair led the Tennessee offense back onto the field. He moved the

Titans into scoring position with the clock ticking away. On the game's last play, McNair passed to Kevin Dyson, who stretched for the goal line. Incredibly, he was tackled just a few feet short as time ran out. To this day, it is one of the Super Bowl's most fantastic finishes.

**LEFT**: Eddie George barrels into the end zone during Super Bowl XXXIV.
**ABOVE**: Kevin Dyson comes up just short of the end zone as time runs out.

# Go-To Guys

To be a true star in the NFL, you need more than fast feet and a big body. You have to be a "go-to guy"—someone the coach wants on the field at the end of a big game. Oilers and Titans fans have had a lot to cheer about over the years, including these great stars ...

## THE PIONEERS

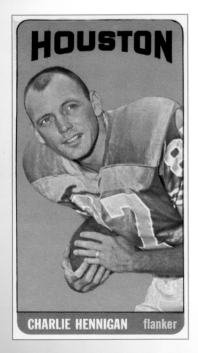

HOUSTON

CHARLIE HENNIGAN    flanker

### CHARLIE HENNIGAN                    Receiver

- BORN: 3/19/1935    • PLAYED FOR TEAM: 1960 TO 1966

Charlie Hennigan was a speedy receiver who got stronger late in games. He was the first player to catch 100 passes in a season. In 1961, Hennigan had 1,746 receiving yards—a record that stood for 34 years.

### GEORGE BLANDA                    Quarterback/Kicker

- BORN: 9/17/1927    • DIED: 9/27/2010
- PLAYED FOR TEAM: 1960 TO 1966

Many pass defenders in the early days of the AFL were inexperienced. George Blanda had the arm and knowledge to take advantage of them. In 1961, he threw 36 touchdown passes in just 14 games.

## KEN HOUSTON
### Defensive Back

- BORN: 11/12/1944    • PLAYED FOR TEAM: 1967 TO 1972

Ken Houston was the best safety of his *era*. He was big and fast, and tackled opponents very hard. During his career, Houston intercepted 49 passes and returned nine of them for touchdowns.

## ELVIN BETHEA
### Defensive Lineman

- BORN: 3/1/1946    • PLAYED FOR TEAM: 1968 TO 1983

Elvin Bethea used his quickness and power to **sack** the quarterback. In the 1970s, he and Curley Culp gave the Oilers one of the best defensive lines in football history. Bethea was voted into the **Hall of Fame** in 2003.

## DAN PASTORINI
### Quarterback

- BORN: 5/26/1949    • PLAYED FOR TEAM: 1971 TO 1979

No quarterback was tougher than Dan Pastorini. He stood his ground even when a defensive player was inches away from him. Pastorini made the Pro Bowl in 1975.

## KEN BURROUGH
### Receiver

- BORN: 7/14/1948    • PLAYED FOR TEAM: 1971 TO 1981

Ken Burrough was easy to spot on a football field. He was one of the only players ever to wear uniform number 00. Burrough led the NFL with 1,063 receiving yards in 1975.

**LEFT**: Charlie Hennigan
**RIGHT**: Elvin Bethea

## EARL CAMPBELL                                          Running Back

- BORN: 3/29/1955    • PLAYED FOR TEAM: 1978 TO 1984

Earl Campbell stood less than six feet tall but weighed more than 230 pounds. Tackling him was like trying to stop a tank. He rushed for 1,934 yards in 1980 and was named **All-Pro** in each of his first four seasons.

## WARREN MOON                                            Quarterback

- BORN: 11/18/1956    • PLAYED FOR TEAM: 1984 TO 1993

Warren Moon won five championships in the **Canadian Football League (CFL)** before joining the Oilers. No quarterback was better at throwing while on the run. Moon led the NFL in passing yards in 1990 and 1991 and was the AFC's top-rated quarterback in 1992.

## HAYWOOD JEFFIRES                                       Receiver

- BORN: 12/12/1964    • PLAYED FOR TEAM: 1987 TO 1995

For many years, Haywood Jeffires was Warren Moon's favorite target. Jeffires led the AFC in catches each year from 1990 to 1992. His best season was 1991, when he finished with 100 receptions.

## STEVE McNAIR                                           Quarterback

- BORN: 2/14/1973    • DIED: 7/4/2009    • PLAYED FOR TEAM: 1995 TO 2005

Steve McNair was such a great runner that many doubted he could be a good passer in the NFL. He proved them wrong by leading the Titans to the Super Bowl in his third year as the team's starter. In 2003, McNair shared the honor as the NFL's **Most Valuable Player (MVP)**.

## EDDIE GEORGE — Running Back

- BORN: 9/24/1973
- PLAYED FOR TEAM: 1996 TO 2003

Eddie George never missed a game in eight years with the Titans. He gained more than 1,000 yards in every season but one. George was named All-Pro for the third time in 2000 when he rushed for 1,509 yards and scored 16 touchdowns.

## ROB BIRONAS — Kicker

- BORN: 1/29/1978  • FIRST YEAR WITH TEAM: 2005

There was no field goal that was too far away for Rob Bironas to attempt. The longer the kick, the more determined he was to make it. In his first seven seasons, he connected on 16 field goals of more than 50 yards.

## CHRIS JOHNSON — Running Back

- BORN: 9/23/1985  • FIRST YEAR WITH TEAM: 2008

Chris Johnson's mix of power and speed reminded many fans of Earl Campbell. In 2009, Johnson had a season for the ages. He ran for 2,006 yards and 14 touchdowns, including a 91-yarder. After the season, he was voted All-Pro and the NFL Offensive Player of the Year.

**ABOVE**: Eddie George

# Calling the Shots

The Titans have a remarkable coaching history. Some of the most talented and creative people in football have worked for the club, starting with the Oilers' first two coaches. In 1960, Lou Rymkus guided the team to the first AFL championship. The man who coached the team's defense that year was Wally Lemm. He replaced Rymkus in 1961, and the Oilers won the AFL title again. Lemm led Houston back to the AFL title game in 1967.

The Oilers had two truly legendary coaches during the 1970s and 1980s. Sid Gillman was known as an offense genius, but he knew a thing or two about defense, too. He took over Houston when the team had the worst defense in the NFL. In one season, the Oilers went from 1–13 to 7–7. Bum Phillips followed Gillman. By the end of the 1970s, the Oilers were one of the best teams in football. Phillips was known for wearing a big cowboy hat and saying funny things to reporters.

In 1994, the Oilers made Jeff Fisher their coach. He rebuilt the team as it moved from Texas to Tennessee. In 1999, he led the Titans to the Super Bowl for the first time. Under Fisher, Tennessee

Jeff Fischer chats with his quarterback on the sidelines.

was known as a very physical team. The Titans also had a fun way of winning games in the final seconds.

After making the playoffs four times in five seasons, Fisher was asked to rebuild the Titans again. He did an excellent job. In 2008, Tennessee returned to the top of the AFC South with a 13–3 record—the best in the NFL. After 17 seasons, Fisher turned the team over to Mike Munchak. He had been an All-Pro lineman for Houston. One of his first calls was to Bruce Matthews, a friend and former teammate. Munchak asked Matthews to join his coaching staff. Together, they began laying the plans for Tennessee's return to the Super Bowl.

# One Great Day

Vince Young had not been in the NFL for very long when the Titans met the New York Giants late in the 2006 season. Maybe that was a good thing. No one had told Young that winning a game when your team is losing 21–0 in the fourth quarter is nearly impossible.

The comeback began with less than 14 minutes left on the clock. After Tennessee intercepted a pass, Young went to work and moved the Titans to the New York 4-yard line. He then threw a pass to Bo Scaife for a touchdown. The score was now 21–7.

The Titans played good defense and forced the Giants to punt. Six plays later, Young scored on a one-yard run. The score

was now 21–14 with less than six minutes remaining. The Titans got the ball back on their own 24-yard line. Young made two great runs and completed three passes. He finished off the drive with a touchdown toss to Brandon Jones. The score was now tied.

The Giants tried to move into range for a field goal, but the Titans intercepted another pass. With time for just a few plays, Young completed two passes to get the Titans into New York territory. Rob Bironas kicked a field goal for a 24–21 victory. Young had led the greatest fourth-quarter comeback in team history.

# Legend Has It

## Was Warren Moon the team's most talented quarterback?

**LEGEND HAS IT** that he was. Moon set a team passing record with 3,338 yards in his first season, and then broke his own mark several times. In 1990, he led the NFL with 4,689 passing yards, including an amazing 527 in one game! He led the league in passing again in 1991 and set a record with 404 completions. Moon's career was long and impressive. He started it in the Canadian Football League and played for three more teams after leaving the Oilers. When you add his NFL and CFL numbers together, he passed for 70,553 yards—by far the most in pro football history.

**ABOVE**: Warren Moon tosses a pass on the run.

# Did the Oilers help lead to the use of instant replay in the NFL?

**LEGEND HAS IT** that it they did. In the 1978 **AFC Championship Game**, the Oilers trailed the Pittsburgh Steelers by seven points when Dan Pastorini threw a perfect pass to Mike Renfro in the back of the end zone. Officials did not think that Renfro had both feet in-bounds when he caught the ball and ruled the pass incomplete. The Oilers lost the game—and their chance to go to the Super Bowl. A television replay showed that Renfro's catch was good. The following season, the NFL decided to let officials look at replays to help them make difficult calls.

# Which player was named after his shoes?

**LEGEND HAS IT** that Billy Johnson was. Johnson returned kicks and punts for the Oilers in the 1970s. In seven seasons in Houston, he scored seven touchdowns on returns. Fans loved his funky end zone dances and the bright white shoes he wore on game days. Johnson was known far and wide as "White Shoes."

The Titans have had some fantastic finishes since moving to Nashville, but fans are still shaking their heads about the end of the team's first-round playoff game in 1999. The Titans hosted the Buffalo Bills. Tennessee led 15–13 in the fourth quarter, but the Bills kicked a field goal with 16 seconds left to take the lead.

Tennessee fans were heartbroken. Coach Jeff Fisher knew his team had one last shot. As the Bills prepared to kick off, he told his team to run a special return play called "Home Run Throw-Back." Lorenzo Neal caught the kick and began running with it. When Neal saw a wall of tacklers coming toward him, he handed the ball to Frank Wycheck. The Tennessee tight end paused for a moment, and then turned to his left and threw a **lateral** all the way across the field to Kevin Dyson.

Neal and Wycheck were not fast runners but Dyson was. There was just one Buffalo player on his side of the field, and he slipped when the ball was in the air. Dyson sprinted past him and ran 75 yards for the game-winning touchdown. The Titans went on to beat the Indianapolis Colts and Jacksonville Jaguars to win their first AFC crown.

Kevin Dyson has three blockers as he races down the field
for the Music City Miracle.

Nashville was a country music town before Tennessee's incredible play against Buffalo. Ever since, it has been an NFL town, too. Titans fans call their fantastic victory over the Bills the "Music City Miracle."

# Team Spirit

In the late 1970s, Houston fans became famous for the ways they supported the Oilers. During games, they often shouted, "Luv Ya Blue!" They drove around the city with bumper stickers that had the same phrase and also wore Oiler-blue clothes and painted themselves Oiler-blue for games.

The players found out how much the fans loved them after Houston lost the 1978 AFC Championship Game. When the Oilers flew home, more than 50,000 fans were waiting to greet them. It was a Luv Ya Blue! party that the players never forgot.

Football fans in Tennessee have continued this tradition of loyal support. They have created a special bond with the Titans. That includes Tennessee's team colors. The Titans—and their fans—continue to proudly wear the color blue.

**LEFT**: Keith Bulluck meets and greets Tennessee fans.
**ABOVE**: This yearbook celebrated the team's 30th anniversary.

In this timeline, each Super Bowl is listed under the year it was played. Remember that the Super Bowl is held early in the year and is actually part of the previous season. For example, Super Bowl XLVI was played on February 5, 2012, but it was the championship of the 2011 NFL season.

**1961**
The Oilers win their second AFL title in a row.

**1980**
Earl Campbell leads the NFL in rushing.

**1960**
The Oilers win the first AFL championship.

**1971**
Ken Houston returns four interceptions for touchdowns.

**1990**
Warren Moons leads the NFL with 33 touchdown passes.

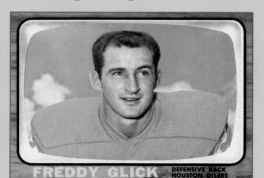

FREDDY GLICK — DEFENSIVE BACK HOUSTON OILERS

Freddy Glick intercepted four passes for the 1961 Oilers.

Ken Houston

OILERS

KEN HOUSTON • S

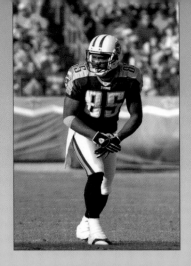

Derrick Mason was a star for the Super Bowl team.

Kerry Collins was voted to the Pro Bowl for his 2008 season.

**2000**
The Titans reach the Super Bowl for the first time.

**2008**
The Titans finish with the NFL's best record.

**2009**
Chris Johnson runs for 2,006 yards.

**1997**
The team moves to Tennessee and becomes the Titans.

**2003**
Steve McNair is named NFL co-MVP.

**2011**
Mike Munchak becomes the team's coach.

Mike Munchak was an All-Pro during his playing days.

## LUCKY 14

During his career with the Oilers and Titans, Bruce Matthews was picked to play in the Pro Bowl 14 times. That set a record for offensive players.

## A TRUE TITAN

In 2011, the Titans named Mike Munchak head coach. It was his 30th season with the team as a coach and player. During the 1980s and 1990s, Munchak played guard and was named All-Pro 10 times.

## WEMBLEY TONI

Before Toni Fritsch was a kicker in the NFL, he was a soccer star for the national team of Austria. In 1965, Fritsch scored twice against England in London's Wembley Stadium to lead his team to victory. After that, everyone called him "Wembley Toni."

**ABOVE**: Bruce Matthews prepares to snap the ball.
**RIGHT**: Tony Banfield

## GOT YOU COVERED

In the early days of the AFL, teams loved to pass. Players who could cover the top receivers were few and far between. Tony Banfield was one of the best. He intercepted 21 passes from 1961 to 1963 and was **All-AFL** each year for the Oilers.

**TONY BANFIELD**
HOUSTON OILERS    DEF. HALFBACK

## FREAK OF NATURE

Jevon Kearse was so big, fast, and *coordinated* that teammates nicknamed him the "Freak." When he spread either of his hands, his thumb and pinkie were more than a foot apart.

## FORCE OF ONE

No defensive player in team history had a better day than Vernon Perry did in the 1979 playoffs against the San Diego Chargers. He intercepted four passes and blocked a field goal in a 17–14 victory.

## CANNON BALL

One of the best players in team history was Billy Cannon. In a 1961 game, Cannon ran for 216 yards and caught passes for 114 more.

# Talking Football

EDDIE **GEORGE**

"We pride ourselves on being able to run the ball."

▶ **Eddie George,** *on the Titans' rushing attack*

"My running style was kind of just head-on."

▶ **Earl Campbell,** *on why he chose to barrel over defenders*

"He doesn't realize it, but he's one of the most respected and popular figures in the country. He's a great role model."

▶ **Haywood Jeffires,** *on Warren Moon*

"We're going to play hard, and if someone doesn't like the way we play, then so be it."

▶ **Jeff Fisher,** *on the team's reputation for being physical*

"He played with unquestioned heart and leadership and led us to places that we had never reached, including our only Super Bowl."

▶ **Bud Adams**, *on Steve McNair*

"Earl may not be in a class by himself, but whatever class he's in, it doesn't take long to call the roll."

▶ **Bum Phillips**, *on Earl Campbell*

"Anytime I'm on the field and my teammates are on the field with me, I just want them to have fun."

▶ **Chris Johnson**, *on not taking the game too seriously*

**LEFT**: Eddie George
**RIGHT**: Bum Phillips

# Great Debates

**P**eople who root for the Titans love to compare their favorite moments, teams, and players. Some debates have been going on for years! How would you settle these classic football arguments?

### Eddie George was the team's greatest running back ....

… because he smashed into the line for tough yards season after season without missing a single start. The Titans used George like a battering ram, but he showed up every Sunday ready for more. In seven seasons with the club, he gained over 1,000 yards six times and was voted to the Pro Bowl four times.

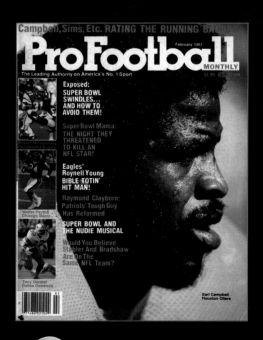

Campbell, Sims, Etc. RATING THE RUNNING BACKS

ProFootball MONTHLY
February 1981
The Leading Authority on America's No. 1 Sport
$1.95

Exposed:
SUPER BOWL
SWINDLES…
AND HOW TO
AVOID THEM!

Super Bowl Mania:
THE NIGHT THEY
THREATENED
TO KILL AN
NFL STAR!

Eagles'
Roynell Young
BIBLE TOTIN'
HIT MAN!

Raymond Clayborn:
Patriots' Tough Guy
Has Reformed

SUPER BOWL AND
THE NUDIE MUSICAL

Would You Believe
Stabler And Bradshaw
Are On The
Same NFL Team?

Walter Payton
Chicago Bears

Tony Dorsett
Dallas Cowboys

Earl Campbell
Houston Oilers

### Earl Campbell was the definition of greatness ....

… because from the first day he stepped on an NFL field, he was the best player in the league. Campbell (LEFT) led the NFL in rushing in his first three years and was named the league's Offensive Player of the Year each season. Campbell was one of the toughest players in history to tackle. It usually took two or three defenders to bring him down.

## George Blanda's Oilers would beat Steve McNair's Titans ....

… because Houston won the AFL championship in 1960 and 1961. Blanda was a smart and talented passer with lots of sure-handed receivers. He was also an excellent kicker under pressure. Billy Cannon, Dave Smith, Charlie Hennigan, and Charlie Tolar would run all over the Titans. The defense—led by Don Floyd and Tony Banfield—would be able to handle McNair.

## Sorry, but Steve McNair's Titans would be unstoppable against those Houston teams ....

… because he had too many weapons for them to deal with. Not only could McNair (RIGHT) outrun and outgun the Oilers, he could always hand the ball to Eddie George, who was as big as the Houston linebackers. As for Blanda, he'd have Jevon Kearse in his face all day, because no one on those 1960s teams would be able to block him.

The great Oilers and Titans teams and players have left their marks on the record books. These are the "best of the best" …

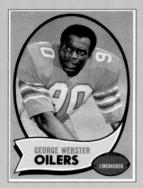

George Webster

Jevon Kearse

## TITANS AWARD WINNERS

| WINNER | AWARD | YEAR |
|--------|-------|------|
| Lou Rymkus | AFL Coach of the Year | 1960 |
| George Blanda | AFL MVP | 1961 |
| Wally Lemm | AFL Coach of the Year | 1961 |
| George Webster | AFL Rookie of the Year | 1967 |
| George Webster | AFL All-Star Game Defensive MVP | 1969 |
| Robert Brazile | NFL Defensive Rookie of the Year | 1975 |
| Billy Johnson | Pro Bowl MVP | 1976 |
| Earl Campbell | NFL Offensive Rookie of the Year | 1978 |
| Earl Campbell | NFL Offensive Player of the Year | 1978 |
| Earl Campbell | NFL Offensive Player of the Year | 1979 |
| Earl Campbell | NFL MVP | 1979 |
| Earl Campbell | NFL Offensive Player of the Year | 1980 |
| Warren Moon | NFL Offensive Player of the Year | 1990 |
| Eddie George | NFL Offensive Rookie of the Year | 1996 |
| Jevon Kearse | NFL Defensive Rookie of the Year | 1999 |
| Steve McNair | NFL co-MVP | 2003 |
| Vince Young | NFL Offensive Rookie of the Year | 2006 |
| Chris Johnson | NFL Offensive Player of the Year | 2009 |

## TITANS ACHIEVEMENTS

| ACHIEVEMENT | YEAR |
|---|---|
| AFL Eastern Division Champions | 1960 |
| AFL Champions | 1960 |
| AFL Eastern Division Champions | 1961 |
| AFL Champions | 1961 |
| AFL Eastern Division Champions | 1962 |
| AFL Eastern Division Champions | 1967 |
| AFC Central Champions | 1991 |
| AFC Central Champions | 1993 |
| AFC Champions | 1999 |
| AFC Central Champions | 2000 |
| AFC South Champions | 2002 |
| AFC South Champions | 2003 |
| AFC South Champions | 2008 |

**ABOVE**: Vince Young was named Rookie of the Year in 2006.
**LEFT**: Warren Moon was the NFL's top offensive player in 1990.

# Pinpoints

The history of a football team is made up of many smaller stories. These stories take place all over the map—not just in the city a team calls "home." Match the pushpins on these maps to the **Team Facts**, and you will begin to see the story of the Titans unfold!

# TEAM FACTS

**1** Nashville, Tennessee—*The team has played here since 1998.*

**2** Memphis, Tennessee—*The team played here as the Tennessee Oilers in 1997.*

**3** Tiffin, Ohio—*Bill Groman was born here.*

**4** Suffern, New York—*Keith Bulluck was born here.*

**5** Atlanta, Georgia—*The Titans played in Super Bowl XXXIV here.*

Toni Fritsch

**6** Raleigh, North Carolina—*Bruce Matthews was born here.*

**7** Orlando, Florida—*Chris Johnson was born here.*

**8** Bartlesville, Oklahoma—*Bud Adams was born here.*

**9** Tyler, Texas—*Earl Campbell was born here.*

**10** Houston, Texas—*The team played here as the Oilers from 1960 to 1996.*

**11** Sonora, California—*Dan Pastorini was born here.*

**12** Petronell-Carnuntum, Austria—*Toni Fritsch was born here.*

# Glossary

🧠 **AFC CHAMPIONSHIP GAME**—The game played to determine which AFC team will go to the Super Bowl.

🧠 **AFC SOUTH**—A division for teams that play in the southern part of the country.

🧠 **AFL CHAMPIONSHIP GAME**—The game that decided the winner of the AFL.

🧠 **ALL-AFL**—An honor given to the best players at each position in the AFL.

🧠 **ALL-PRO**—An honor given to the best players at their positions at the end of each season.

🧠 **AMERICAN FOOTBALL CONFERENCE (AFC)**—One of two groups of teams that make up the NFL.

🧠 **AMERICAN FOOTBALL LEAGUE (AFL)**—The football league that began play in 1960 and later merged with the NFL.

🧠 **CANADIAN FOOTBALL LEAGUE (CFL)**—A professional league in Canada that began play in 1958.

🧠 *COORDINATED*—The ability to have all body parts work well together.

🧠 *DECADES*—Periods of 10 years; also specific periods, such as the 1950s.

🧠 **DIVISION**—A group of teams that play in the same part of the country.

🧠 **EASTERN DIVISION**—A group of teams that play in the eastern part of the country.

🧠 *ERA*—A period of time in history.

🧠 **FIELD GOAL**—A goal from the field, kicked over the crossbar and between the goal posts. A field goal is worth three points.

🧠 **FUMBLES**—Balls that are dropped by the players carrying them.

🧠 **HALL OF FAME**—The museum in Canton, Ohio, where football's greatest players are honored.

🧠 **INTERCEPTIONS**—Passes that are caught by the defensive team.

🧠 **LATERAL**—A toss of the ball backwards.

🧠 *LOGO*—A symbol or design that represents a company or team.

🧠 *MERGED*—Joined forces.

🧠 **MOST VALUABLE PLAYER (MVP)**—The award given each year to the league's best player; also given to the best player in the Super Bowl and Pro Bowl.

🧠 **NATIONAL FOOTBALL LEAGUE (NFL)**—The league that started in 1920 and is still operating today.

🧠 **OVERTIME**—The extra period played when a game is tied after 60 minutes. A second overtime period is called double-overtime.

🧠 **PLAYOFFS**—The games played after the regular season to determine which teams play in the Super Bowl.

🧠 **PRO BOWL**—The NFL's all-star game, played after the regular season.

🧠 *PROFESSIONAL*—Paid to play.

🧠 **ROOKIE**—A player in his first season.

🧠 **SACK**—Tackle the quarterback behind the line of scrimmage.

🧠 **SUPER BOWL**—The championship of the NFL, played between the winners of the National Football Conference and AFC.

🧠 *TRADITIONS*—Beliefs or customs that are handed down from generation to generation.

🧠 *VETERANS*—Players with great experience.

# OVERTIME

**TEAM SPIRIT** introduces a great way to stay up to date with your team! Visit our **OVERTIME** link and get connected to the latest and greatest updates. **OVERTIME** serves as a young reader's ticket to an exclusive web page—with more stories, fun facts, team records, and photos of the Titans. Content is updated during and after each season. The **OVERTIME** feature also enables readers to send comments and letters to the author! Log onto:

**www.norwoodhousepress.com/library.aspx**

and click on the tab: **TEAM SPIRIT** to access **OVERTIME**.

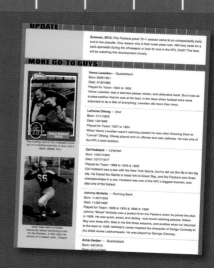

Read all the books in the series to learn more about professional sports. For a complete listing of the baseball, basketball, football, and hockey teams in the **TEAM SPIRIT** series, visit our website at:

**www.norwoodhousepress.com/library.aspx**

## On the Road

**TENNESSEE TITANS**
1 Titans Way
Nashville, Tennessee 37213
615-565-4000
www.tennesseetitans.com

**THE PRO FOOTBALL HALL OF FAME**
2121 George Halas Drive NW
Canton, Ohio 44708
330-456-8207
www.profootballhof.com

## On the Bookshelf

To learn more about the sport of football, look for these books at your library or bookstore:

- Frederick, Shane. *The Best of Everything Football Book.* North Mankato, Minnesota: Capstone Press, 2011.

- Jacobs, Greg. *The Everything Kids' Football Book: The All-Time Greats, Legendary Teams, Today's Superstars—And Tips on Playing Like a Pro.* Avon, Massachusetts: Adams Media Corporation, 2010.

- Editors of *Sports Illustrated for Kids. 1st and 10: Top 10 Lists of Everything in Football.* New York, New York: Sports Illustrated Books, 2011.

# Index

PAGE NUMBERS IN **BOLD** REFER TO ILLUSTRATIONS.

## About the Author

**MARK STEWART** has written more than 50 books on football and over 150 sports books for kids. He grew up in New York City during the 1960s rooting for the Giants and Jets, and was lucky enough to meet players from both teams. Mark comes from a family of writers. His grandfather was Sunday Editor of *The New York Times,* and his mother was Articles Editor of *Ladies' Home Journal* and *McCall's*. Mark has profiled hundreds of athletes over the past 25 years. He has also written several books about his native New York and New Jersey, his home today. Mark is a graduate of Duke University, with a degree in history. He lives and works in a home overlooking Sandy Hook, New Jersey. You can contact Mark through the Norwood House Press website.

ML                    10-15